day moon rising

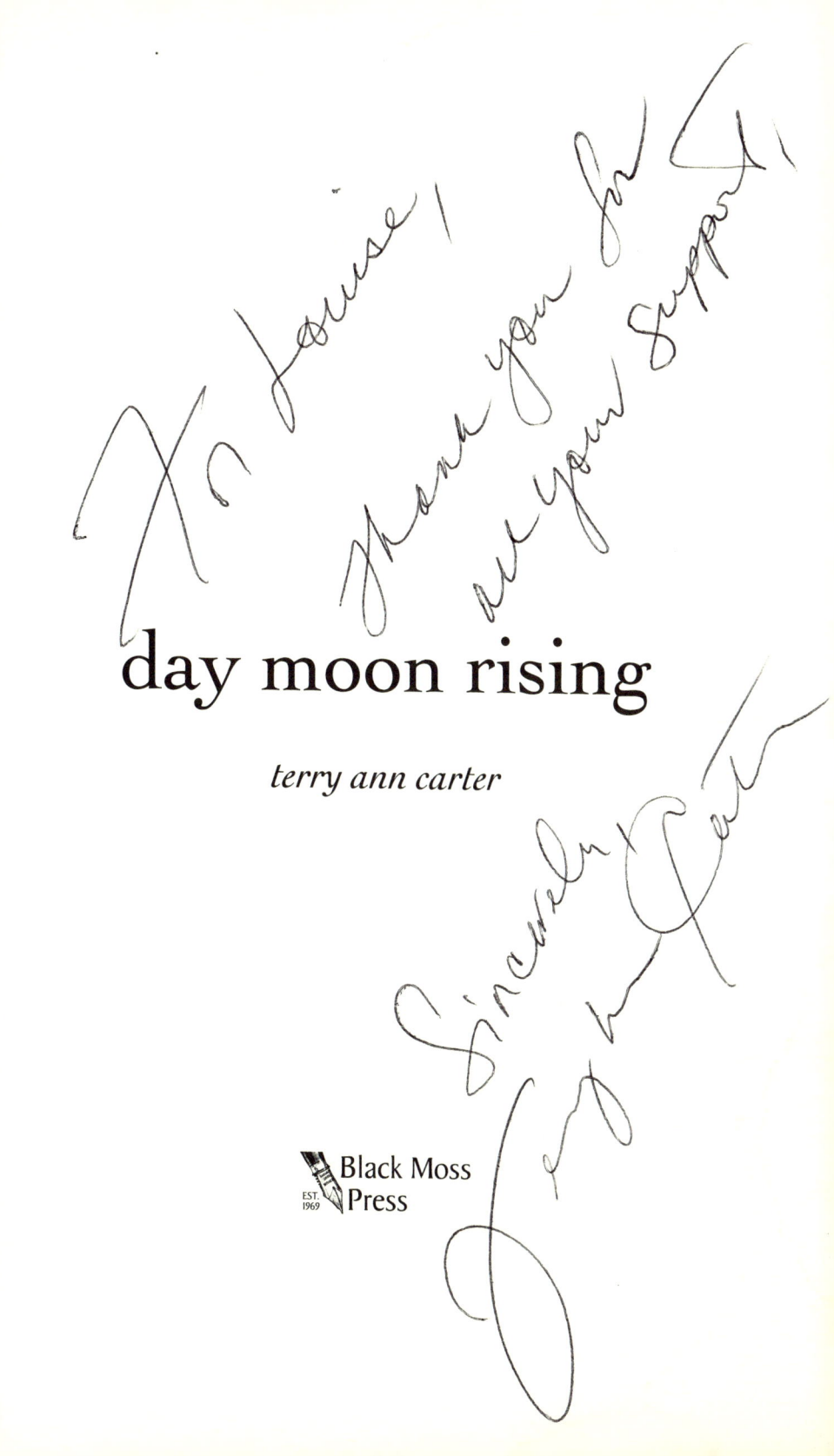

day moon rising

terry ann carter

Black Moss Press
EST. 1969

Copyright © 2012 Terry Ann Carter

Cataloguing information available through Library and Archives Canada

ISBN 978-0-88753-499-7

Cover photo: Marty Gervais
Interior design: Nicole Leclair, Christina Strangio, and Victoria Faraci
Cover design: Samantha Alfini, Krysten Bortolotti, and Syed Qaiser Kamal Ahmed

 Black Moss Press

Published by Black Moss Press at 2450 Byng Road, Windsor, Ontario, N8W 3E8 Canada. Black Moss books are distributed in Canada and the U.S. by LitDistCo. All orders should be directed to LitDistCo. Black Moss Press books can also be found on our website www.blackmosspress.com.

 Canada Council for the Arts / Conseil des Arts du Canada

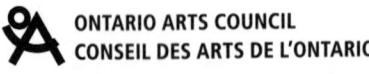 ONTARIO ARTS COUNCIL / CONSEIL DES ARTS DE L'ONTARIO

Black Moss would like to acknowledge the generous financial support from both the Canada Council for the Arts and the Ontario Arts Council.

PRINTED IN CANADA

*for Janne Ritskes
& Somaly Mam*

The Tabitha Foundation of Canada works side by side with the people of Cambodia, reaching out to the despairing in their communities. Tabitha's current program affects one percent of the Cambodian population; presently over 300,000 people in twelve provinces in the country. Since 1994, Tabitha has lifted more than one and a half million Cambodians out of poverty and despair, into lives of dignity, hope, and active participation in their communities. I am pleased that Terry Ann Carter's poems will sing Tabitha's song; that poetry lovers around the world will hear the music of good work.

Janne Ritskes
Tabitha-Cambodia
#239, Street 51, P.O. Box 2361
Phnom Penh, Kingdom of Cambodia

at this moment

early dusk, starlings swerve/ after rain	13
curl of incense smoke/ water urn	14
At This Moment	15
What a Spirit House Wants	16
Faith	17
Picture a Woman	18
Prayer for Somaly Mam	19
Rotten	20
Much like Absence Much like Missing	21
For the Tuk Tuk Drivers	22
Phnom Penh: April 17, 1975	23
Year Zero	24
Bury Me Deep	25
monks chanting / killing fields	26
in the glass case/ spirit house	27
cloudless/ going steady	28

a thousand dragonflies

house building/ the street singers' music	31
the silence between us	32
Unaccustomed As I Am	33
Where Does What Matters, Begins: Part one	34
Janne's House Building Rules	36
Where Does What Matters, Begins: Part two	37
A Woman From the Village Steps Forward	38
A Thousand Moments Before I Entered This Village	39
Sweetness in My Belly	40
A Toast	41
dragonfly's glitter/ pond	42
through the dragonflies' wings/ white bones	43
village path/ white orchid	44

edge of rain

temple doorway/ hibiscus blossoms	47
Moult	48
Sonnet 18	49
Mr. Toc Bin Shoots Off More Than His Mouth	50
Dragon Fruit	51
Travelling in the Tropics	52
The Dance, Like Syntax, Continues to Spin	54
Morning	55
Guesthouse: Names of Geckos, Names of Love	56
Temperature Rising	58
Night Market	59
Banteay Srei	60
Lacquered Red	61
Clear Light	62
temple hallway/ at the guest house	63
Cambodian dusk / Banteay Srei temple	64
Angkor	65
acknowledgements	66
notes	70
about the author	72

prologue

Wild Lotus
(after Mary Oliver)

You do not have to be vigilant.
You do not have to be aware of every little sign.
You do not have to record the millions buried.
It is an insurmountable task.

You can't set down the facts.
You can't go ghost
hunting in the fields of mines.
You can't even say you have a stake
in this harvest.

Whoever you are
know that the wild lotus
that blooms in the filth of ponds,
is pure.

When I say here I mean
the ringing of a Buddhist bell.
Light opening a red camellia.
Bones of children buried in killing fields.
Day moon rising.

at this moment

early dusk
starlings swerve
through the sound of temple bells

after rain
the monk's yellow umbrella
points to the sky

curl of incense smoke
the hotel owner's
crooked grin

water urn
the candle's flicker
drowns itself

At This Moment

Incense smoke drifts, spins. Unravels
in the air scented with sandalwood,
sliced ginger. Lobby of the Golden Gate Hotel

No. 8, Street 278, Phnom Penh.
Beneath a basho leaf a hundred spiders
move slowly on their threads.

Grenade parts, AK 47s, photocopied girlie
mags in the Russian market. Stacks of silk.
Prostheses.

Turning mid-air
a flock of starlings.
Under a yellow umbrella, two monks

glide off the curb. Stop to light incense
at the spirit house on the corner
between the gas station and the foreign

book store. A small ceremony of remembrance.
At this moment my mind swings
like a Nikon 84.

When I say here:
I mean the ringing
of a Buddhist bell.

Light opening a red camellia.
Bones of children buried in killing fields.
Day moon rising.

What a Spirit House Wants

A spirit house wants to be called
by its proper name: *san phra phum*
wants to celebrate the dead.

A spirit house wants to be blessed
by a holy man, in consultation
with its owner.

A spirit house wants the offerings
of families: bananas, coconuts, mango
set on tiny steps.

To be an invitation
for the closed palms of prayer.
Close to orchids, basho leaves,

a spirit house wants
to remind the world
of day and night ceremonies.

Small remembrances.
Curl of incense smoke
unravelling into sky.

Faith

A man pays money to have sex
with a virgin, purifies himself
of the AIDS infection. Her pale
face above the stalk of her body.
Every kind of bruise visible.

The girl loves her blue and white
school uniform, asks if there is a God.
She believes that if she cuts her arm
mixes her blood with another's
she will not be alone in her suffering
will not be alone in her death.

Picture a Woman

Here mercy rings a bell. Her presence
a miracle. White walls. White chairs. Sun

illuminates the darkest corners. Picture
a woman bending over the youngest child.

Picture a woman waiting for medical
reports. Spinning words into laughter.

Picture a woman invoking
the gods. Endless days.

Boundaries of rock, vast floods of
charity. Picture the only woman to come ashore.

The hurt of children like boats paddling
upstream, lifting out of white water.

Prayer for Somaly Mam

I've spent the morning immersed in your book.
Wounds open like black blossoms,
the moon swims in every one.
I know you can imagine this world invisible,
an instinct honed on the flood of your own
desire to set things right. To abolish evil.

From which all exiled ones will return home.
The beasts of your memory rising: sold into
slavery at the hand of your grandfather, now,
who could you trust? Your beaten face
a small star. You have chosen to live here,
Phnom Penh, city of your childhood.

Listen, whatever it is you are trying to do,
the children you rescue will sing again.

Rotten

There are streets in Phnom Penh
you never enter, never cross

into the memories of childhood...
the black and blue air of brothels

stink of sex on a tattered mattress.
Men came and went all night

even in morning their heat
burned your legs and armpits.

And if you ran away,
betrayal of the worst kind

slugs embedded beneath your skin
slimy monsters in your hair.

>You remember Svak Pa Village.
>Thousands of girls in tar papered shacks.
>
>Pink florescent lights.
>Cardboard walls.
>
>When a child has been torn
>over and over in the dark
>
>she dreams of death, of fresh air rising
>above her heart.

Much Like Absence
Much Like Missing

Because a tuk-tuk driver has gone
to get her, a child may enter this shelter
at any moment: Bleeding. Black. Blue.

Because she is addicted to drugs
and could be sold for mere dollars.
Because she has been burned.

Because she may have dysentery, AIDS,
TB. Because she is eight years old.
Because if she dies, she wants to die here.

For the Tuk Tuk Drivers
(after Edward Hirsch)

Tonight I want to speak about
the tuk tuk drivers who have
so much faith in their navigation,

who know these roads like a crab
knows sand. Three wheeled taxi,
auto rickshaw, the canvas roof

and drop-down sides, convenient
in rainy seasons. I love the way
they are willing to go off the path,

find the gravel roadway to a family
temple. Just out of town.
Always they know the best restaurants.

Can recommend fried beef
with green mango. Spicy duck salad.
Fish amok in baby coconut shells.

Still in communist style. We pass
a poster celebrating the tenth anniversary
of Khmer Rouge demise. *Evil,* my driver says,

My father buried in killing fields.
I love the tuk tuk driver who carries
a *stop sex trades in south east asia* sign.

I trust he will wait for me.
Carry me.
Home.

Photograph, Phnom Penh: April 17, 1975

Your eye notices the rock faces
of young Khmer Rouge soldiers

marching wide boulevards. Skulls
wrapped in krama headscarves.

Ammunition brazen against chests.
Something unspoken, unfamiliar.

Something pouts. Like a prostitute.
In the upper left hand corner

a young woman raises her arms –
on another day she might gather

lotus from the ponds outside the city
carry stalks to street corners

to sell. Today she whispers
freedom, five years of civil war

come to an end. Sunlight spills
over trees, floods the city centre.

This is where the revolution will begin.
Teachers, tailors, civil servants, monks

you can almost see them hiding
you know what history has in store.

This photograph has a title:
Year Zero – negative space.

Year Zero

> *To keep you is no benefit. To destroy*
> *you is no loss.*
> (Khmer Rouge ideology)

This placid countryside converted
by diabolical propaganda, somewhere

a heart is missing a beat. Pol Pot,
Brother Number One, of all your atrocities

the plunder of children the most
unforgivable: the low sounds in their throats

as they turned in their families.
Under your instruction they executed

their own. I hold my breath, lungs
filled to bursting. Your poison

still, in this air. In Tuol Sleng Prison
the bloodied rooms left intact.

Bury Me Deep
(for New Zealand collage artist Kate Northcott)

When my head has been severed
and my face lost in tunnels

when my back can no longer
bear the strike of torches

and the yellow moon looks down
in disapproval. When my arms

and legs have become entangled
with a thousand other limbs

and my belly has been emptied
of blood, then bury me deep

in the dirt of killing fields
so rain may wash the bones

of my skull, and the wind
may sing me whole.

monks' chanting
in the temple
and beyond

             killing fields
the wind carries a butterfly
          bone over bone

in the glass case of skulls,
a reflection
of my own face

                              spirit house
                           at the hair salon
                            I light incense
                             for my mother

cloudless
the outstretched palms
of begging children

going steady
with the tuk tuk driver
spring moon

a thousand dragonflies

house building
my hammer's echo
against hollow bamboo

the street singers' music
a thousand green dragonflies
hum in the sky

the silence
between us
steaming green tea

Unaccustomed As I Am
(for Kate Braid)

I do not know the power of weight,
the ease to drive nails. I have not found

my rhythm on the hollow bamboo floor.
I do not know the cold powered steel

the hickory grain, titanium ti-bone, curved
long, straight, rip claw, curved claw, drywall,

sledge. The setting hammer, raising hammer,
finish, framing. I have not studied

the carpenter's course. I do not mix cement.
Yet, in Prey Veng jungles, western Cambodia

I am part of a house building team,
will bandage wrists and thumbs to haul stilts,

bend tin to wrap around walls. My handsome
Estwing, forged from metal, leather wrapped,

clangs by mid-day, echoes in air filled
with dragonflies, scent of white orchid.

I am trying to keep sweat
out of my eyes, my mind off water break.

Where Does What Matters, Begin: Part One

Three blocks from the Golden Gate Hotel.
No. 239, Street 51. Headquarters of Janne
Ritskes. Founder of Tabitha. Leader. Mother.

In her second storey outdoor office we are
points of a mandala. Intent in our listening
the sun sears our eyes. A canvas cloth

raises and lowers according to the hour.
Janne's orientation speech: the KR bloody takeover,
Vong's story, a girl at the time of invasion

if only I could have kept the babies alive, Janne,
I am bad. I am bad.
She knows this talk by heart. It is her heart.

I look past Janne's shoulder, past the shoulders
of women seated on the cement floor, AIDS
patients from the city, quilting blocks of yellow,

blue, bits of cotton from the exchange bin.
Khmer chatter flies in all directions.
I'm aware of my adult children here,

seated in the circle, the cloudless Cambodian sky
hovering over us, aware of the shy teenaged girl
I used to be, listening to Bob Dylan, believing in karma,

never knowing where it would take me.
Where does what matters, begin?
I see my life come shining

from the west down to the east.
I close my eyes, holding it all in.
My children. The circle. The talk. The sky.

Any day now, any day now
I shall be released. On my deathbed
it will be the last moment I see.

Janne's House Building Rules

Janne lays down the law with her stern
smiling face: *Do not share your food
with the Cambodian people. It will give them
wobbly tummy.*

Do not walk around with your tops off.

*Tip water over your head every half hour
this is to prevent heat stroke.*

*No sex. No drugs. No rock and roll.
Learn about this culture. Practice "Namaste".*

Do not hold or touch babies.

*If you hit your hand with a hammer, do not
make a fuss. It is not about you. It is not about you.*

Where Does What Matters, Begin: Part Two

A finished house takes a team of volunteers
six hours to build: four stilts, four walls, a roof.
Our muscles lean into the strive of nails.

The geckos' click clack. By mid-day we glisten.
Hammers down, we notice the sky filled with them.
Dragonflies. Thousands. All possible shapes waiting

to come into being. As if these nearby orchids
blooming in spires of white breath, might change
the gravitational bend of light. Bamboo huts.

Sheltered hovels. Children sleep in string
hammocks, eat green papaya melons.
Soon they will sit on their steps

green tin wrapping around them.
The sun spins faster at the equator.
Where does what matters, begin?

A Woman From the Village Steps Forward

Performance art. Here, I might call it village art.
A woman steps forward sunlight spilling from trees.

She removes the red and white chequered Tabitha
karma from my neck. Lowers it to a cistern of water.

By mid-day, a push of heat. We shine like
the gecko's clack. Every insect stirring in dirt.

The woman from the village wraps wet cloth
around my head. Her scarred hands a cup.

Like all good theatre, I am apart yet a part
of this play. Revolutionary.

Her own krama forced on villagers
at the scourge of Pol Pot.

Her tongue makes little clicking sounds.
The critic of my soul. Raves.

A Thousand Moments Before
I Entered This Village

The space between me and the woman
from the village who has stepped forward
is filled with prayers, with airports,
silk lampshades, glasses of red wine.
Photographs of my children at play.
Later, their travels around the world.
My husband waiting in our bed.

With palms together *Namaste. Namaste.*

Chumm riep sur, suk sabai.

Sweetness In My Belly

The villagers wait to see
if I will accept the gift.
A taste of sugar palm, strained

through a red and white krama.
Our translator explains
preparations were made this morning.

One of the men climbed thirty feet
to reach the fruit at the top.
All natural, the translator beams.

She knows I have come
from far-away. *KAN - A - DA*
she whispers.

I take a sip. The women giggle
behind their hands. Heat
and red dust everywhere.

A Toast
(after Pamela Porter)

I raise my glass
to the Cambodian countryside
lifted and glorified by wind
to the men and women working in fields
bent over rice, over cane
visible on the horizon.

To the new houses built on stilts
wrapped in corrugated tin
the crawl spaces beneath
where hammocks will stretch
nestlings for dark haired angels
who watch us with furrows
in their foreheads.

Here's to the Canadian woman, Janne Ritskes,
who told her mother at five years old
I want to bring cookies to the poor.

To my sons, who believe in Tabitha's
work. My husband, most magnanimous
in spirit, "may we wander this world,
 expecting nothing, recording everything."

dragonfly's glitter
the sound of water
over the cistern's rim

pond
in first light
the low hum of bees

through the dragonflies' wings
the sky
bluer

                                                                                 white bones
                                                             of something small
                                                       ants crawl in and under

village path
a red and white krama left
on the bicycle

white orchid
in its center
my center

edge of rain

temple doorway
all our shoes
in one pile

hibiscus blossoms
girls paint their nails
for the tourists

Moult

At the edge of rain. On the verge
of being sick. The slight rumination
in the bowel that forbids wellness.

I practice the art of insect watching
take my mind to the nature of things.
Cicadas dragging thoraxes through dust.

Beetles, shining green and gold against
pale lichen. I lean my elbows against
the window sill, dissect the diaspora

of ants climbing a basho leaf.
Everything sluggish, as though
even rain could not wash away

this scent of dead skin.

Sonnet 18 Revisited

Shall I compare thee, Lonely Planet, to
Fromer, Fodor, Rough Guides, Let's Go, and more
You are more friendly and more versatile
With facts to document and show these paths
Less traveled. I am most fortunate to have
Your pages with me: if chance or nature's changing
Course may alter plans, I will not falter.
For thy eternal wisdom shall not fade
For travel is a cure: the heart is hooked.
You will be steadfast with the visa rules
I can depend on all that I have booked.
On this I find the winding road to home.
    So long as pilgrims breathe or eyes can see
    So long lives Lonely Planet's gift to me.

Mr. Toc Bin Shoots Off
More Than His Mouth
> *no coincidence Colonel Kurtz lived in Cambodia*
> Lonely Planet Guide

You can't believe the stories in your guide book.
Phnom Penh in the 1990's. A wild west of south east Asia.

Take for example, the story of Mr. Toc Bin. Drug smuggler.
Asking his body guard to remove an AK 47 from the trunk
of his car.

Mr. Bin walks down the tarmac. Shoots a tire off the plane
that brought him from Bangkok.

> *they give such poor service —*
> *if they were my employees*
> *I'd have shot them in the head*

Police acknowledge the actions were illegal.
Concede they have no plans for prison.

Dragon Fruit

To tell if a dragon fruit is ripe
place your hands over the black
barbed fins, press into the centre.
If it is soft the pink flesh will drip
into your palms an ointment to cure
the broken heart on your sleeve.
Black seeds scatter like rain.

You could write a children's book about
the history of dragon fruit, illustrate it
with short line drawings in ink.
Create characters in a morality play.
The bad guy with the longest nose.

Like ancient Khmers before you
before Buddha, before Shiva, who worshipped
spirits, alive in the veins of leaves. Roadside dust.
You could fall on your knees. Pray to dragon fruit.

You could gather them off the buffet table
in the restaurant of the Golden Gate Hotel.
Carry them to your room on the sixth floor
to place on the shelf above the porcelain
sink. A feast for the tiny red ants that keep
pestering you for food. You could block
the leaky air con. Compose a blues riff
on your Hohner harmonica. Slide yourself silly.

Traveling in the Tropics

In some far off place, say, Siem Reap,
Cambodia, in a small guest house

along the Siem Reap River, travellers rest
for twelve dollars US. Drink Apsara beer.

I removed my shoes one moonlit night
to walk across tiles, the skin of my feet

leaving a trail of phosphorescent glitter
like the luminata of some ancient fish

swimming the ocean floor of my room.
Or temple spirits coming down

from Angkor Wat, searching for new companions.
Their ghostly flesh imprinted on cool terra cotta.

Later I dreamt of you, the years between us
flowing like calligraphic ink down scrolls.

I remember not what we are now,
but what we were.

How we began moving
toward each other.

> In the heat of this tropical night
> mosquito nets stick to placid walls
>
> I remember the ice house you carved
> from snowy bricks.
>
> The way you laid them down
> one on top of the other

>blowing against your fingers
>to keep them warm.

The way you lit it from within.
Calling me. To come and look.

The Dance, Like Syntax, Continues To Spin

These poses determine the story. Dancers
rely on a system of intricate cues. Imagine

the palms, splayed fingers turned
to the light, bending backwards over

themselves. Legs positioned – just so.
Arms, too, in the telling of Buddhist

tales. Love. Loss. Sacrifice.
Words cannot hold the sound

of cymbals, nasal reediness of *sralai*,
that oboe pitch measured

in lengths of breath. Inhale. Exhale.
Lift of left foot. Language is useless

in the seamless magic of movement
called dancing, yet carries its message

in the curving body
lifting itself from pain.

Morning

I am here. You are there.
An entire world between us.

I slip into this cavern of thought
watch the day moon rise slowly.

Over temple tops. Gold domed pleasure
of palaces.

Guava juice out of a tea bowl.
Bird songs I don't recognize.

An old woman carries leeks, limes
in a string bag, her crippled steps slower

in the onslaught of traffic.
The mind is a magnet.

yellow plumeria
orange hibiscus

bird of paradise
Your love pulls me

in all directions.
Do I need to say more?

Guesthouse: Names of Gecko, Names of Love

I hear others move night after night
even sneezes or the sounds of love
someone sick at the sink.

A phone rings. No one answers.
We are strangers here except
for a table of books in the front hall

stories that connect us like pilgrims.
Now the other voices: wail of siren.
Bark of the neighbour's dog.

Even a rooster's call that wakes me
before first light. The echo of tricycle wheels
on the cool cracked tiles of the hall.

I find a grey-green gecko
on the bathroom floor.
Startled. I listen in the humid dark

to the housekeeper
move up and down the stairs with a broom.
What are the names of *gecko*

in other languages: Russian, Swahili
French? In Indonesian it is *tokek*
like the click clack sound

of a percussion player, dropping
castanets. In some regions, seven echoes
in the night air: tokaaay… tokaaay… tokaaay…

On the guesthouse television
a carp flaps its tail sending
ripples across the surface of a pond.

At home, in the heart of winter
the aurora borealis spreads its petals
across the sky.

This I have come to know –
the bending of a pine bough
another name for love.

Temperature Rising

Thirty nine degrees in the shade, even
cicadas quiet. The fans, sticky
in their turning. The barman sweats
like the glasses he serves.

I remember the mysterious fruit
in a Kahlo painting, a kind of prickly pear
imagine her making guacamole for Rivera
and black beans. For dessert: papaya –

scraping the seeds with their tongues.
From this restaurant window
looking out at the Quay, the banks
of the Sonle Tap in full view

I see an egret stretch into its long warp
like this day, unfolding.
A monk sweeps debris from the palace steps.
Across the city, at the Bodi Tree Café

across the street from Tuol Sleng Prison
tourists sit dazed, with cold drinks
in their hands, trying to forget images.
Heat makes rivulets of fire down sleeves.

Frieda's brush
like the egret's wings, like the torturer's
whip, marks air: more terrible
more true than this heat.

Night Market

I savour the noisy Siem Reap night markets
stalls of silken scarves and lemongrass
the flash of jewellery hung on bamboo racks
smells of curried fish balls, braised tripe

skewers of squid or scallop. Dumplings.
My body bathed in smoke and spices.
I'm amused by the outdoor tubs – *happy spa*
tiny fish gathered from the Tonle Sap

that nibble dead skin from the flesh of feet.
The whoops of high pitched laughter.
Vendors selling purses, frogs, baseball bats
embroidered dolls with lacquered faces

leather shoes, mattresses, kitchen clocks.
Labyrinth of laces, meat cleavers, paper
cranes folded into strands for hanging.
Chimes. Opium pipes. Fresh fruit.

My mind wanders with the swirl and
rush of it. The breadth and width of it.
Warrens of sand carvings, key chains
with Angkor temples, chubby Buddhas.

Baskets of bracelets, the jingle jangle
of it. Long necked shadow puppets
and dragon fruit, those fins like
feral beasts ready to defend

the defenceless.
In the night market, I am lost
in the merriment of here
the indescribable joy of now.

Banteay Srei

Of all the temples in Angkor
and there must be at least forty –

Banteay Srei is my favourite:
I imagine the fingers of women

holding the implements to carve
pink sandstone, quartz arenite into

small delicate roses trailing lintels.
Foliage. Female dancers, perfect

in proportions. Their loosely draped skirts
and heavy earrings almost moving

in an intimate gesture toward friendship.
This is a thing you need to touch

as though tapping these secrecies would
breathe life into cold stone.

A blessed mood erases the wasted
fields, the blood soaked earth of earlier

roads. I am reminded of the Buddhist proverb:
the fallen flower never returns to the branch

the broken mirror never again reflects.
I close my eyes to recall a favourite haiku –

the falling flower
I saw drift back to the branch
was a butterfly

the chakra of my spine, split open.

Lacquered Red
> *I want to live a life of lacquered red*
> John Brandi

Outcry from some lonely bird
I cannot name, the sky

as Sisley would have painted it –
prepared to pour. The heart is a frog

ready to splash into pond water
the afternoon unbends like lily pads

floating on long flimsy stems.
Old stones seem to be weeping.

I am nose to nose with dripping basho
leaves, their scent like crystals

in a darkened cave. How can I explain
this longing for crimson, the brick-red roofs

of Spanish houses, rouged lips of orchids.
Just below the surface of my eyes, I search

for hibiscus coloured birds, for russet sunsets,
radish flavor in every plant I eat.

For the Queen of Hearts. Rose-pink shrimp
on silver trays, the swirl of a ruby skirt.

In a Rothko painting
I want to be the vermillion streak.

> Below this Cambodian courtyard, I conjure a man
> who presses his palm into the small of my back
>
> his left leg against my thigh. In tempo with temple bells
> we tango into the lacquered red.

Clear Light

A dragonfly hovers over the small cistern
of water. It waits for a chance to land.

The courtyard patio overlooks a crowded road
sleepy in this afternoon's haze.

The dragonfly, luminous, catches each ray.
Deciphers it within its body.

How like this insect I want to be, taking light
to the darkened edges of the world.

Let things shine.

temple hallway
where monks have walked
the echo of my bare feet

at the guest house
a gecko
makes himself welcome

Cambodian dusk
the calligrapher's brush
holds an image
for only a moment
before it dries

Banteay Srei temple
women practice tai chi
by the lotus pool

Angkor
finally, stone
has the last word

acknowledgements

The following poems placed second in the Great Blue Heron Poetry Contest and appear in *Antigonish Review*, autumn 2011:
"At This Moment"
"For the Tuk-Tuk Drivers"
"Traveling in the Tropics"
"Dragon Fruit"
"A Woman from the Village Steps Forward"

"Year Zero" was published as a broadsheet by *Rideau Ferry Press* for the Tree Reading Series, 2003.

"Traveling in the Tropics" was published in *Ice Floe*, University of Alaska Press, under the title "Dreaming Ice Floes."

"Lacquered Red" was published in *a wall's sharp white* (Tree Press/Phafours press, 2011).

Some of the haiku first appeared (some in earlier versions) in the following journals and anthologies:
Frogpond
A Travel-Worn Satchel: The Haiku Society of America Members' Anthology
Yomiuri Daily Times (Japan)
Haiku Canada Review
Stillness (Ming Editions, Montreal)
such green (pendas poets, London, Ontario)
Riverwind (Hocking College, Nelsonville, Ohio)
Matrix (the Zen Issue)
Observer Observed, Haiku Canada Members' Anthology
Lilliput Review

Anthology of English Language Haiku by Women, edited by Aubrie Cox.
The Temple Bells Stops: Contemporary Poems of Grief, Loss and Change, edited by Robert Epstein
A Monk's Fine Robes: A Haiku Sequence from Cambodia, Leaf Press
Now You Know (hexagram series) King's Road Press
The following poems under the title "Haiku from Cambodia" won the Origami Crane Award For Best Poem, 2010. "water urn," "temple doorway," "killing fields," "in the glass case," "darkening clouds," "empty sky," and "going steady."

I would like to thank:
Marty Gervais, of Black Moss Press, for his unflinching belief in this book and for my work in Cambodia.

Canada Council for the Arts and the Ontario Arts Council for generous grants to complete these poems.

The editorial team at Black Moss who worked so diligently on this book: Syed Qaiser Kamal Ahmed, Samantha Alfini, Krysten Bortolotti, Jason Bortolotti, Laryssa Brooks, Victoria Faraci, Jaclyn Klapowich, Jessica Knapp, Nicole Leclair, Kristina Storey, Robert Craig Visser, Christina Strangio, Sylvia Pham, Jordan Turner and Kate Hargreaves. Thank you for making magic.

Mary Ann Mulhern: my Black Moss partner and good friend.

The Ottawa (M)other Tongue poets for good critiquing sessions and friendship over the years: Sylvia Adams, Susan Atkinson, Frances Boyle, Barbara Myers, Claudia Coutu Radmore, Peter Richardson, Guy Simser, Paul Tyler, Gillian Wallace, Margaret Zielinski.

Betsy Struthers, fellow traveller in this part of the world, who first glimpsed these poems and offered support and enthusiasm.

KaDo Ottawa haiku poets for eleven years of haiku promotion: Claudia Coutu Radmore, Philomene Kocher, Mike Montreuil, Guy Simser, Sheila Ross, Heather Taylor, Betty Warrington Kearsley, Grant D. Savage, Sheila M Ross, Melanie Noll, Pearl Pirie. May we always find time to share coffee and our latest poem.
Mr. Toshi Yonehara who supported Ottawa KaDo with annual spring meetings at the Embassy of Japan.

Tabitha Board of Canada – supporters in all activities relating to Tabitha: Bob Carver, Paula Piilonen, Lucia Dolcetti, Luanne Doner (retired), Yolanda Henry, Lisbeth Mousseau, Colin Eades (retired) and to volunteers Wendy Cunning and Marilyn Eades.

Jennifer Kightley Carter, my beautiful daughter-in-law, who first introduced me (virtually) to Somaly Mam.

House Building team (2009) in Prey Veng province - teachers from United World College of South East Asia (Singapore): Chris Davies, Rehema Munting-Davies, Vicky Tilbury, Hew Tranter, Kymaree Sheather, Tony Dealy, Rachael Lewis, Laura Chapman, Carrie MacDonald, Kari Twedt, Shannon Westgate, Sonia Matthews, Stephen Rowcliffe, Dylan Carter and Jennifer Kightley.

House Building team (2011) in Prey Veng province – teachers and friends of United World College of South East Asia (Singapore): Dylan Carter, Jennifer Kightley Carter, Barrett Carter, Michelle DuGuay, Arti, Emma Crombie, Jasmine Coope, Caroline Stannard, Geraldine McGrath, John

McGrath, Andrea McDonald, Simon Bignell, Kevin Crombie, Sonia Matthews.

House Building Team "Hammers for Homes" (2011) in Kep: Yolanda Henry, Dennis Kam, Kathy Heit, Carole Matheson, Andrew Matheson, Michele Darling, Michael Eagen, Tracy Kam, Riley Kam, Robin Pascoe, Sunny Eades, Pat Chiota, Lys Urquizo plus our team mates "Aussies on Harleys" Chris Zammit, Alain Costeroste, and Xavier Glenard, also known as the "Orange Riders".

Darryl, Dylan and Barrett Carter: my compasses home.

notes

"What a Spirit House Wants"
Buddhism is the dominant religion in Cambodia and was the state religion until 1975, when the Khmer Rouge took control of the country. During 1975 – 1979, the vast majority of Cambodian monks were murdered by the Khmer Rouge who also destroyed the country's 3,000 wats (temples). Since the 2000's – monks, with their alms bowls, and spirit houses have become common sights again. Spirit houses are places for ancestor worship.

"Faith"
"By far the lowest statistic for the number of prostitutes and sex slaves in Cambodia is between 40,000 – 50,000. It can be expected that at least 1 in 40 girls born in Cambodia will be sold into sex slavery" (2005 report by Future Group, a Canadian nongovernmental organization)

"Prayer for Somaly Mam"
Somaly Mam is the author of *The Road of Lost Innocence,* a memoir. Sold into slavery by her grandfather at sixteen, Somaly survived unspeakable acts of brutality; today she rescues, rehabilitates, and reintegrates sex workers (some as young as five and six years old.) Somaly lives in Cambodia. More information regarding her work may be found at www.somamly.org

"Photograph: Phnom Penh: April 17, 1975"
April 17, 1975 was the date of the Khmer Rouge "invasion" of Phnom Penh. After five years of civil war, the citizens welcomed the soldiers. By the end of the day, the tone of the city had changed, as two million people were forced to leave in marches to the countryside. The sick and disabled were left to die on the roadside. Many were sent to labour camps

scattered throughout the country. More information about this historic day, and the KR regime can be found in the following: *How Pol Pot Came to Power* and *The Khmer Rouge Regime* by Ben Kiernan, *Brother Enemy* by Nayan Chanda.

"Year Zero"
Saloth Sar, better known as Pol Pot, Brother Number One, leader of the Khmer Rouge, became leader of Cambodia in mid 1975. During his time in power he imposed a version of "agrarian socialism", forcing urban dwellers to relocate to the countryside to work in collective farms and forced labour projects, toward his goal of "restarting civilization" in "year zero." The combined effects of forced labour, malnutrition, poor medical care and executions, resulted in the deaths of nearly two million Cambodians. Some reading about this period includes: *The Killing Fields* by Sydney Schanberg and Dith Pran, *The Gate* by Francoise Bizot.

"Where Does What Matters, Begin: Part One"
The Tabitha Foundation is a non-profit, non-denominational organization that seeks to reach out to the despairing in their communities and enable them to address their needs in a holistic and sustainable way. Tabitha was founded by Janne Ritskes in 1994. The foundation includes: a savings program, a cottage industry program, house building programs. There are chapters of the Tabitha Foundation in Canada, the U.S.A., Australia, New Zealand, Singapore, and U.K. You can find more information about the Tabitha Foundation (Canada) at www.tabitha.org

"Banteay Srei"
"the falling flower" is a haiku by Arakida Moritake.
More interesting reading about the temples: *Angkor – An Introduction to the Temples,* by Dawn Rooney, and *Angkor – Heart of an Empire* by Bruno Dagens.

about the author

Terry Ann Carter is the author of four books of poetry: *Waiting for Julia*, Third Eye Press, 1999; *Transplanted*, Borealis Press, 2006; *A Crazy Man Thinks He's Ernest in Paris*, Black Moss Press, 2010; and *Hallelujah*, Buschekbooks, 2012. Her poems have appeared in numerous journals including *Arc*, *Vallum*, *Dandelion*, *Antigonish Review*, *The Windsor Review*, *Matrix*, *Carleton Arts Review*, *Grey Borders*, *Nexus*. A dozen anthologies contain her work, the most current, *Pith & Wry: Canadian Poetry*, Your Scrivener Press, edited by Susan McMaster.

An internationally recognized haiku and tanka poet, Carter has won awards for her Japanese literary forms. She is President of Haiku Canada; in 2011 she published *Lighting the Global Lantern: A Teacher's Guide to Writing Haiku and Related Literary Forms*, Wintergreen Studios Press. She placed first in the Great Canadian Haiku Contest (2011) and won the Origami Crane Award in 2010.

As past Chair of the Tabitha Foundation (Canada) her humanitarian work has taken her to Cambodia for house building expeditions, and field work. Carter has served the League of Canadian Poets as Education Chair and presently as Ontario rep. She was the Random Acts of Poetry poet for the city of Ottawa, (2005 – 2010).